GUIDES TO EVERYTHING

GET A GOOD NIGHT'S
Sleep

By Linda Bird

ISBN 978-1-84678-004-2

Copyright 2006, Quick123 Limited

Quick123 Limited, PO Box 45092, London N4 2ZJ.

Website: www.quick123.co.uk

Customer service or additional copies can be sought at service@quick123.co.uk.

• QUICK123 GUIDES TO EVERYTHING •

Letter to the Reader

Sleep, when you get enough of it, is utterly delicious. It helps keep you healthy, happy, sane and ready to tackle anything.

However, if statistics are anything to go by, few of us are getting enough sleep at night and we are suffering as a result. You know how even one night's disrupted sleep can dampen your mood, affect your performance at work and blow all sorts of worries and anxieties out of proportion.

I used to consider myself naturally a poor sleeper. It would always take me hours to drift off, and I would wake up tired and lacklustre. If I couldn't drop off, I'd calculate how many hours' sleep I'd probably get and worry that I wouldn't be able to function the following day on so little rest. Then I was making things worse by indulging in long lie-ins at the weekend.

Now I have three small children and have experienced true sleep deprivation, which has made me realise that even five or six hours' unbroken sleep a night is a luxury.

I'm more convinced than ever that having sufficient sleep can transform your life and that everyone can achieve a better night's rest with the right expertise. That is why I have written this book.

I've explored the reasons why so many of us are not waking up refreshed and the best tricks and techniques to help you get a good night's sleep without resorting to drugs.

This could be just what you bleary-eyed people out there have been waiting for. Try it tonight.

Sweet dreams

Linda Bird

Contents

Quick123 Limited
PO Box 45092
London N4 2ZJ

Email: peterpurton@quick123.co.uk

Dear Quick123 reader

Thank you for buying this guide. We hope you enjoy reading it.

Our aim is to help you achieve the goals you set yourself, whether it's getting a better job, improving relationships or creating a better you. And to help you achieve that without costing you too much time, effort or money.

Because you, the reader, are at the centre of everything we do, we'd like to hear from you. Whether you have comments about this book, ideas for a new topic or issues in your life you feel we might be able to help with, send us an email or a letter.

If we take up any of your ideas to create a new title we'll make sure you get your own special copy.

We want to provide you with the kinds of guides you want to read. With your help, I'm sure we can.

Happy reading,

Peter Purton
Quick123 Limited

The great sleep deficit

How did you sleep last night? Not all that well, if statistics are anything to go by. Studies show that about 40 per cent of women and 30 per cent of men in the Western world are seeking help for sleep problems, and that one in five of us consults our GP at one time or other because of some kind of sleep disorder.

Perhaps you rarely sleep well, and are one of the millions who suffer from insomnia – a prolonged inability to get sufficient, restful, uninterrupted sleep. Apparently as many as one third of adults do, and sufferers are more likely to be women, or those over 60.

Perhaps you just have difficulty falling asleep when you are troubled by the stresses and strains of work and family life.

Perhaps you are a light sleeper who has difficulty staying asleep, and are woken by the slightest noise.

Do you simply just not get enough hours' rest, and continually wake up too early in the morning, feeling un-refreshed? For many of us, the problem isn't in getting to sleep, and staying asleep, we are simply choosing to stay up working or playing too hard.

So, how much sleep is really enough?

The optimum

Research shows the optimum amount of sleep tends to be somewhere between six and a half and eight and a half hours a night.

Most people, about two thirds of us, sleep for that kind of period each night. Less than twenty per cent of us get less than that and 16 per cent sleep for longer.

The big question is, what is right for you? Sleep experts say the best gauge is to ask yourself if you are waking up each morning feeling refreshed. Are you able to function at your best? If so, you're probably getting enough.

If not, you need to get to the root of your sleep deficit. Try keeping a sleep diary to assess how you are feeling each day.

"Studies show that 40 per cent of women and 30 per cent of men in the Western world are seeking help for sleep problems"

If you need a stiff coffee to liven you up, then you could need more sleep.

Vital repairs

Sleep is so important to our health and wellbeing because vital repair work goes on when we are asleep.

As you pass through the stages of sleep, your body's growth hormone is produced which helps all your cells repair and regenerate. Sleep enables our mind to process the day's events and activities. It boosts your immune system and makes your body less vulnerable to infections and viruses.

"As many as one third of adults suffer from insomnia and sufferers are more likely to be women, or those over 60"

Research also shows that getting a good night's sleep can help boost memory, and let newly formed memories and skills get organised in the brain. Without it, your brain just doesn't function effectively.

We all know how lacklustre and lethargic we feel when we've had a bad night, and how a series of late nights or disturbed sleep can damage our physical, mental and emotional wellbeing.

Lifestyle

While a short course of sleeping pills may be helpful to some, many of us would prefer a drug-free alternative.

Modern drugs are not as addictive and habit-forming as their predecessors, but some drugs cause side effects such as dizziness, headaches and feelings of agitation.

Also, coming off sleeping tablets abruptly may trigger a recurrence of insomnia and some drugs do not mix well with other prescription medication.

A healthier and more lasting alternative to drugs is to overhaul your lifestyle. There are a host of natural solutions to many sleep problems. The first step is to identify the cause of your particular sleeping problem.

Skimping on sleep can also cause weight gain. When you are tired, your willpower is weakened, so you are more likely to reach for fatty, sugary or salty foods, and to skip that exercise session.

Accidents

Some studies have shown that losing just one and a half hour's sleep for one night can reduce your alertness in the daytime by as much as 32 per cent.

Another study found that people who went to bed six hours later than their normal bedtime performed as badly in terms of their attentiveness and reactions as those who were legally classifiable as drunk.

Sleep deprivation has also been linked to accidents. Chernobyl and the Challenger shuttle explosion are high profile examples, and thousands of accidents take place every year as a result of tiredness.

Then there's the emotional fallout from continuous lack of sleep – relationship strife, parenting problems, ineffectiveness and discontent in the workplace can all stem from fatigue.

Health and beauty

Insufficient sleep is associated with other, more serious health issues. Too few hours can, for example, increase your risk of developing diabetes.

Research shows that women who get fewer than five hours' sleep each night increase their risk of getting diabetes by a third. One reason could be because the lack of sleep may reduce levels of the hormone that tells you to stop eating.

Even short bouts of sleep deprivation can raise blood pressure, pump extra stress hormones into your bloodstream and raise blood sugar levels.

There are cosmetic issues to consider too. Lack of sleep can age you, as it contributes to the breakdown of collagen in the skin and makes blood vessels more visible, which causes those dark lines under your eyes.

"Research shows the optimum amount of sleep tends to be somewhere between six and a half and eight and a half hours a night"

How good - or bad - a sleeper am I?

I find it difficult to fall asleep.

I can't stop the thoughts racing through my mind; they keep me awake.

It takes me at least half an hour to get to sleep at night.

I often feel afraid to go to sleep.

I worry about things and find it hard to relax.

I wake up in the night and can't get back to sleep.

I usually sleep all night, but never feel refreshed in the morning.

I wake up earlier in the morning than I'd like.

I wake up in the morning with stiff and aching muscles.

I often feel down and depressed, and lacking in energy.

My legs often twitch during the night.

I often tend to nod off at inappropriate times during the day.

If you answered yes to three or more of the above statements, you could be suffering from insomnia and need to look at your sleep patterns.

What's causing your sleep problems?

Isolating the problem will help you find a cure. The truth is, often there's more than one cause for sleep disruption. Here are a few common ones.

Age: experts say sleep problems increase as we get older; studies show that, during the peri-menopause (the transition to menopause), up to 42 per cent of women experience problems sleeping. A 65 year old is one and a half times more likely to complain of insomnia than a 45 year old.

Plus, conditions such as sleep apnoea (repeated blocking of the airwaves at night), restless leg syndrome and insomnia are more common in the over forties. Adopting good sleep habits can help you adjust to different sleep patterns as you get older.

Hormonal fluctuations: women often find sleep patterns are affected during puberty, pregnancy and the post-partum period. PMS sufferers may also suffer regular sleep disruption.

Too many stimulants: caffeine is thought to remain in your body for 12 hours, which disrupts the quality of your sleep. Caffeine is found not only in coffee, but also in colas, tea and chocolate. Alcohol is another stimulant. It may temporarily make you drowsy, but it actually shortens the time you spend in the deeper stages of sleep and may make you wake up in the night.

Smoking: nicotine is a powerful stimulant and can trigger adrenaline, which keeps you alert. Studies show smokers take twice as long to drop off as non-smokers, and sleep half an hour less.

Sedentary lifestyle: being a couch potato can actually contribute to sleep problems. Regular exercise can help you fall asleep more easily, and sleep for longer. One study showed that low levels of physical activity are linked to a higher risk of chronic insomnia in later life.

Bad sleep hygiene: many of us just do not have a positive sleep environment. Taking work to bed, watching television under the covers, eating or snacking in bed, a too-hot or too-cold room, even the wrong colour bedroom walls can all contribute to poor sleep.

"Many of us just do not have a positive sleep environment"

Worry: stress and anxiety are major causes of insomnia. Stress hormones deplete the feel-good hormones serotonin, melatonin and GABA (gamma-amino-butyric acid), creating a vicious cycle of worry and wakefulness.

Depression: it often goes hand in hand with insomnia, and prolonged lack of sleep can lead to depressive feelings.

Late night over-activity: anything other than sex at bedtime can conspire to keep you awake. Some experts believe that exercising late at night can mean you take longer to fall asleep.

Poor diet: platefuls of additives, junk food and regularly eating on the run don't help either. Try and eat your five fruits and vegetables every day and do not snack on foods that are high in fat or sugar before bed.

Weight: being overweight can cause disrupted sleep. This is because sleep apnoea (where you momentarily stop breathing during your sleep) is more common in overweight people. Sleep apnoea not only makes you feel groggy and un-rested, but is linked to high blood pressure and circulatory problems. One US study showed that losing 10 per cent of your body weight could reduce your symptoms by 26 per cent.

Disruption to routine: jet lag, late nights, early morning meetings, a heavy workload and even lovely holiday lie-ins can prevent a good night's sleep. Routine is the key to good sleep.

Burning that candle: too many late nights and bringing work home will cut down on your relaxation time and lead to sleep deprivation.

What keeps me awake?

The sporadic bad sleeper: if you find that your sleep patterns are dependent on what is going on in your day-to-day life and you can only sleep well when you are on holiday, or if on waking you feel stiff, achy and have a headache, then stress governs your body clock.

Try: relaxation techniques like yoga or meditation.

The too-early riser: if you find yourself waking up very early then finding it difficult to get back to sleep or you find yourself worrying about the state of world peace, which prevents you from getting to sleep, then you have one of two problems. This could be an early sign of depression, though if you haven't been experiencing feelings of hopelessness, anxiety or lack of confidence, then it could be a sign that your body clock is out of kilter.

Try: writing down your worries before you go to sleep or exercising more.

The junk food problem: if you are overweight and rooted to the couch, or go to bed feeling full-up, or hungry, or are a smoker, drinker or junk food fan then your lifestyle is causing your sleep problems.

Try: Cutting out any food that is high in fat, sugar and processed ingredients. Start exercising, eating more fruit and vegetables and generally get healthy.

The candle burner: if you never go to bed at the same time and tend to spend evenings socialising or working and only manage to catch up on your sleep at weekends, then your routine is at the root of the problem.

Try: Going to bed and getting up at the same time every day, even weekends.

The comfort conundrum: if you cannot get comfortable in bed – you are too hot or too cold and cannot stop fidgeting – or you use your bed for everything: reading, working, eating, watching television, then you need to reorganise your bedroom.

Try: Reassess what you use your bedroom for – it should be a sanctuary for sleep. Make sure the only activities permitted in your bed are sleeping and making love.

Create the perfect bedroom for sleep

• •

Your night's sleep is only as good as your sleeping environment, but there are plenty of ways to optimise this without moving home. One of the most effective things you can do is organise your bedroom.

Keep it cool

Leave the window open. The optimum bedroom is well ventilated and completely dark (so invest in blackout curtains in summer). The best temperature for sleep is about 16-18 degrees C – cold enough to require a blanket. Invest in a babies' room thermometer to keep your bedroom at its optimum temperature.

"Studies show those who are exposed to sounds while sleeping may release stress hormones such as cortisol even when they're asleep. Cortisol is linked with premature ageing"

Keep it quiet

Try a set of ear plugs. Studies show those who are exposed to sounds while sleeping may release stress hormones such as cortisol even when they're asleep. Cortisol is linked with premature ageing and can deplete your immune system. Ear plugs can reduce noise by 50 per cent so are good investments if your partner or the neighbours are conspiring against you.

If the noise still bothers you, try moving into a back bedroom if you live on a main road. If you're woken mid sleep cycle – a sleep cycle lasts about one and a half hours – by outside noise, it makes you feel very sluggish, and leaves you with a hangover feeling.

Thick lined curtains or blinds help minimise outside noise. Try a thick carpet; it can dampen sounds by up to 12 times compared to bare boards.

"Try redecorating your bedroom with pale green, which is considered a restful colour"

Keep it uncluttered

A clear, tidy room is more restful than a cluttered one. Every day have a 15 minute tidy up – not directly before bedtime as it may be too stimulating.

Put tomorrow's outfit out for the morning; make sure dirty clothes are in the laundry basket.

Nothing should be on the floor and all surfaces are clear. You're aiming for a clear, airy room.

Keep it restful

Try redecorating your bedroom with pale green, which is considered a restful colour. Avoid reds, oranges and yellows and brightly patterned wall paper, all of which can be over-stimulating.

"Medium to fim mattresses are best and should be changed every 10 to 15 years"

Pale blue may also help you relax. The colour blue was first found to lower blood pressure back in the fifties, when it was suggested as a natural tranquilliser, so use colours like pale blue, pale green or soft turquoise to make a small, cramped bedroom feel more spacious.

Remove books, papers and paraphernalia from surfaces; keep them in bedside tables. Eliminate

disturbing sounds and light; cover illuminated numbers on the alarm clock, for example.

Create the ideal bed for sleep

Keep your bed fairly simple. Rather than tons of pillows, stick to crisp sheets in natural fabrics and colours.

Sprinkling lavender oil on the pillow or lavender linen spray on the sheets may help as lavender is a natural sedative and relaxant.

Medium to firm mattresses are best and they should be changed every 10 to 15 years. A good mattress doesn't sag when you're lying on your side. Your spine should be parallel to the mattress.

Don't use too many pillows as these throw your head out of alignment. Keep the huge puffy ones for decoration only.

Cotton pyjamas are better than silk ones, because silk doesn't move with your body so well.

De-clutter your mind

Keep a bedtime worry book by the bed; it is ideal if a maelstrom of must-dos keeps invading your mind. Write them down and forget about them until tomorrow.

Wise Words

Spring clean your bed

Make your bed as comfortable and inviting as possible. Start by turning the mattress, get your duvet and bedding cleaned and scent sheets with a fabric spray.

White bed linen is perfect as it looks cool and clean. Layer different fabrics and textures over your bed to make it look comfortable

Finding the right routine

Sleep experts maintain that it is vital to find, and stick to, a routine. We should all be aiming to get up and go to bed at the same time every night because our body's circadian rhythm (body clock) needs to base itself around a fixed point.

When sleep patterns are erratic, your body constantly resets its circadian rhythm and those fluctuations make it harder to get a really restorative night's sleep.

Make sure you go to bed and get up at the same time every night, or within 30 minutes of it. Your biological clock primes you for sleep between 10 and 12pm and to wake between 6am and 8am.

TOP TIPS

Exam techniques

If you have a vital presentation or exams to study for, and need to put extra hours in, sleep experts say you're better off working later rather than getting up earlier in the morning. Studies show sleeping in the early morning between 2am and 6am is more restful and beneficial than late night sleep (between 10pm and 2am).

Don't make the mistake of thinking you can catch up on your sleep at the weekends by having a lie-in till midday. You'll just disrupt your pattern. Instead, go to bed and get up at the same time every day – even weekends. If you must lie in, allow yourself just an extra hour.

Goodnight dos and don'ts

Establishing a nightly routine that helps you wind down and prepare for bed is vital.

What to avoid

Eating late: it raises your body temperature and keeps your body and brain switched on. Eat early evening – a couple of hours before bedtime. This will cause your metabolism to drop, which will help you sleep.

Alcohol: cut out caffeine and alcoholic drinks within four to six hours of bedtime. Alcohol reduces the amount of time you spend in deeper stages of sleep.

Getting over-stimulated: no vigorous exercise just before bedtime and avoid horror movies or late night television. The only activity you can indulge in is sex. Studies show orgasms release endorphins, which can trigger sleep. Don't work or do anything too taxing before bed; the key is to quieten your mind.

What to do

Allow yourself to wind-down before bed: have a relaxing bath. Use oils like lavender, geranium, jasmine, ylang ylang, rose or sweet marjoram in a bath or in a burner in your room as they have sedative effects.

Pick up a novel: a gentle read helps you wind down and switches off adrenalin production.

Have a warm drink: try camomile tea or warm milk with a spoonful of honey – a natural sedative.

Listen to relaxing music: research has shown that listening to 45 minutes of soothing music every night at bedtime improves sleep quality, helps people sleep longer, decreases the incidence of sleep disturbances and helps people function better during the day.

Try gentle yoga stretching: the deep breathing practised in yoga slows your breathing and heart rate and encourages the body to relax.

Try relaxing your back, shoulders and neck with this move: stand with your feet hip distance apart, knees bent, and bend from the waist so your chest is in contact with your thighs and your arms are hanging down.

Sway gently from side to side, releasing tension in your neck and shoulders. As you inhale, roll your back slowly up, finally bringing your arms over your head. Exhale slowly and curl back down. Repeat 4 times.

Try this bedtime relaxation technique: lie on the floor, arms slightly away from your sides, legs apart and feet hanging to the sides and eyes closed. Make sure your back is flat to the floor and that you are comfortable.

Slow your breathing – feel it go in through your nose, travel into your lungs and out again. Draw your attention to each part of your body, taking a moment to tense, then consciously relax, it. Focus your breathing by counting to four on an inhale and six on the exhale. Remain here for at least a minute.

Keeping a sleep diary

You should be asleep for 85 per cent of the time you are in bed. Filling out a sleep diary for a week or so can help you identify why you wake and what's keeping you up.

Note what you did prior to bedtime — your routine, what time you went to bed, roughly how long it took you to get to sleep and what kept you awake.

Include how many times you woke in the night and how long it took you to get back to sleep. Don't obsess about time as clock-watching makes insomnia worse. Instead, make an estimate of how often you woke and for how long.

Note the time you woke in the morning, work out how many hours you were in bed and how many of those you actually spent asleep.

Detail what you ate and drank that day, and at what time — it may help you identify foods or drinks that are stimulating you too much.

Finally, summarise how you felt on waking, and during that day.

To nap or not to nap

It seems a sensible solution. If you can't sleep at night, shouldn't a lovely afternoon nap leave you more rested?

"A regular daytime nap may not be the best approach for insomniacs, however tired they may feel"

Not necessarily. A regular daytime nap may not be the best approach for insomniacs, however tired they may feel. This is because regular napping can disrupt your normal sleep cycles further and get your body used to sleeping during the day.

"Regular napping can disrupt your normal sleep cycles and get your body used to sleeping during the day"

However, there are times when an occasional nap may be useful – perhaps because you want to be alert for a long car journey or bright-eyed for an important evening work event. A short nap in the afternoon can boost mental performance and get you firing on all cylinders.

Insomnia sufferers can try minimising the adverse effect of an occasional nap on their night time sleep by going to bed later that night; just postpone your bedtime by the amount of time you napped during the day.

Happy nappers

For those of us who don't suffer from chronic insomnia, a short 15-minute power nap in the afternoon has been found to be more refreshing than even one hour's sleep, especially if you take it between one and three when your body is primed for slumber. Many big corporations have 'napping rooms' where employees are encouraged to take a 'microsleep' to enhance their performance during the day.

> **"Good quality sleep involves two different sleep phases, slow wave sleep and rapid eye movement – or 'dreaming' – sleep"**

Short naps do seem to help boost productivity. One study of sleep-deprived people found that those who napped for 10 minutes were more alert three hours afterwards than those who took a 30 minute snooze.

TOP TIPS

Golden rules for a better night's sleep tonight

Follow these top tips from experts at The London Sleep Centre:

1 **Stick to a regular bedtime and wake up schedule**
Aim to go to bed and get up at the same time each night and morning. Don't go to bed too early or you may have trouble falling asleep or your sleep may be restless.

2 **Cut back on naps**
Napping can disrupt normal sleep cycles. Try skipping your nap and see if regular sleep patterns improve.

3 **Make your bedroom a 'quiet room'**
Don't watch television in your bedroom. Keep your bedroom for sleep and sex only.

4 **Establish relaxing before-bed routines**
Have a bath, a glass of warm milk or do some light reading before bedtime.

5 **Develop relaxation techniques**
Try yoga, deep breathing, quiet meditation or listen to soft music while trying to fall asleep.

6 **Avoid troubling news right before bed**
Violence in newspapers or on television may bother some people and make it difficult to sleep. Try reading a book instead.

7 **Avoid stimulants**
Don't have drinks containing caffeine (tea, coffee, cola) less than six hours before bedtime. Avoid alcohol or tobacco; they may calm you at first but they can disrupt your sleep during the night.

8 **Exercise regularly**
It helps the body and mind stay healthy, but avoid vigorous exercise right before bedtime.

Other experts say 45 or 90 minutes is the optimum amount for a nap. The secret seems to be the quality of sleep during that nap. Another study found that those who had a good quality nap performed better in tasks during the afternoon than those who did not have a sleep in the daytime. Good quality sleep involves two different sleep phases: slow wave sleep and rapid eye movement – or 'dreaming' – sleep.

The optimum time for sleep is two hours, which allows you to go through a full sleep cycle (90 minutes) after which you should wake up feeling refreshed. If you wake up mid cycle, you may feel groggy.

Quick123™

•GUIDES TO EVERYTHING•

**We want to hear from you.
Give us your feedback
by emailing us at
feedback@quick123.co.uk**

Easy ways to
boost
your sleep
potential

Is your lifestyle keeping you from enjoying a satisfying, restorative night's sleep? Your weight, exercise habits and stress levels can influence your sleep – or lack of it. Perhaps it's time to make changes to your daily routine.

Eat for sleep: avoid vegetables such as cauliflower, cabbage and broccoli in the evening if you're prone to bloating, as they can make you too uncomfortable to sleep. Try a carb-rich snack before bed-time – carbohydrates release serotonin which helps make you feel relaxed.

Open your curtains in the morning: or go out for a morning stroll. Getting early morning light is said to increase the production of melatonin, a hormone that helps regulate sleep.

Move your body: people who exercise tend to sleep better than sedentary people. Exercise often goes hand in hand with other healthier behaviours, so it will benefit more than your sleep patterns. Some experts maintain that an evening workout could be more effective than a morning one because it primes your body for sleep. Try exercising about three hours before bedtime and your body will cool down before you get into bed.

Go eastern: practising tai chi three times a week for six months has been found to help people sleep longer and more soundly. A daily half-hour yoga session can also help you sleep better.

Wind down with music: tests show that soft music 45 minutes before bed can improve your sleep in about three weeks. Most effective tunes are those with 60 to 80 beats per minute – try Bach's preludes or Beethoven's symphonies.

Offload: stress and anxieties can build up and keep you awake at night. Give yourself a regular 'life audit' – assess how you're feeling, coping, what you want/need to change about your life and then set yourself realistic goals. This will help you to look at your life in a positive way and stop feelings of anxiety from snowballing.

Don't overdo the work: especially if you work at a computer. It seems you sleep better at night if you take small five or ten minute breaks from the screen and stretch, relax and rest your eyes or go for a ten minute walk round the block. Headaches, joint pain and stiff shoulders can be caused by intensive computer work, and can compound sleep problems. Aim for a break every twenty to thirty minutes.

Try counselling: Cognitive Behaviour Therapy has been found to help change insomniacs' negative mindsets about sleep, re-evaluate their bedtime routine and help them adopt new, healthy habits. After eight weeks of therapy, one group of sufferers found counselling significantly more effective than drugs at improving their sleep.

Lose weight: overweight people are prone to sleep apnoea, and snoring, which can disrupt sleep. Keep your weight down by taking three to five half hour sessions of exercise each week, and follow a low fat, low calorie diet.

Wise Words

Exercise isn't just something that the government bangs on about being necessary for school children: it helps your body function better in a variety of different ways. It can help your mind to relax as well as helping to keep your weight down. Both will have a positive effect on your ability to get to sleep

Natural
remedies and
kitchen cures

The idea of taking sleeping pills is usually a last resort for insomniacs. They may treat the symptoms, but don't go to the root of the problem.

Although it's true that many of the drugs for sleep problems aren't necessarily as habit forming as they once were, their benefits are fairly short lived. They may successfully send you to sleep, but often it's not good quality sleep, so isn't so restorative.

Today's pills
Barbiturates were the main solution to sleep disorders fifty or so years ago. They're occasionally still prescribed by doctors now, in the shape of Amytal and Soneryl, and work by helping decrease nerve activity in the brain, which

leads to drowsiness. However they tend to be habit forming and may affect liver and kidney function.

Today, doctors are more likely to prescribe tranquillisers (benzodiazepines such as Ativan and Tranxene). These work by reducing anxiety and helping relax the muscles. Again, these may have side effects, aren't recommended for people with certain health conditions and can also be addictive.

"Tranquillisers work by reducing anxiety and help relax muscles"

The other commonly prescribed classes of sleeping pill are imidazopyridines and cyclopyrrolones; they slow down your brainwaves and relax muscles. Again, there are side effects.

A gentler approach and short-term solution to sleep problems may be one of the many over-the-counter remedies, such as Nytol and Sominex. These contain antihistamines and work by making you drowsy so you fall asleep more easily.

Even with these over the counter medications, there may be side effects – grogginess in the morning, dry mouth and blurred vision – and they're not recommended for those with heart problems, urinary or prostate conditions, or for pregnant or breastfeeding women.

Critics of sleeping medications claim pills only treat the symptoms and don't encourage a natural healthy pattern of sleep. As a result, many prefer natural remedies.

Eat your way to better sleep
A carbohydrate rich meal at the end of the day can help you feel relaxed and sleepy – try a risotto or pasta dish – or even a bowl of milky porridge. Avoid indigestible fatty, meaty or creamy meals.

Avoid sugary foods late at night. They can raise your blood sugar levels, giving you a burst of energy. Magnesium-rich foods have been found to help in fighting depression and low moods and encouraging sleep. Magnesium is found in green leafy vegetables, nuts and wholegrain cereals.

If you are finding it hard to sleep because you're feeling down, or anxious, increase your intake of essential fatty acids. They are found in nuts, seeds and oily fish. Also add vitamin B6-rich foods, such as chicken or sunflower seeds, to your menu.

Have a tryptophan-rich snack before bed. It's been found to help promote sleep and boost morning alertness. Foods that provide a dose of tryptophan include bananas, dairy, nuts, eggs, soya beans, tuna, turkey, cottage cheese, baked beans and chicken. Keep the serving size small and have your snack about an hour before bed.

Some foods contain the feel-good hormone serotonin, which eases anxiety and can boost your mood. Avocados, bananas and tomatoes contain serotonin.

Ditch the caffeine-rich drinks like tea, coffee and even hot chocolate. Instead stick to camomile, lemon balm and passion-fruit tea.

Alternative routes to better sleep
Acupuncture is an effective way to treat sleep disorders. One German study was based on 40

people who complained of difficulties falling asleep or remaining asleep. One group was given a course of acupuncture, the other group a placebo. Results in a sleep laboratory showed an improvement in sleep only in those who received the acupuncture. It is painless and relaxing.

Aromatherapy: this age-old therapy uses oils extracted from plants to help boost health and wellbeing and is an effective way to treat stress and insomnia. Best essential oils for insomnia include neroli, myrtle, sweet marjoram, rose and lavender. Put a drop or two on a tissue and sniff at bedtime, light aromatherapy candles or burn essential oils in a diffuser or light bulb ring.

For a soothing aromatherapy bath, add four to six drops of essential oil to bath water. Add some milk or a drop of vodka to the bath to help the oils disperse. Using oils neat on skin can cause irritation and some may have contraindications.

Try a steam inhalation. At bedtime, add a few drops of oil to a bowl of boiling water, pop a towel over your head and breathe for a few minutes.

Flower remedies: these are tiny homeopathic remedies diluted in water, which are said to help restore the body's emotional wellbeing. Good remedies for sleep problems include oak for exhaustion, olive for extreme physical and mental tiredness, rose for anxiety and nightmares and white chestnut for an over-stimulated mind and sleeplessness. A few drops on your tongue should work.

Acupressure: acupressure stimulates the body's own meridians, the invisible pathways through which energy circulates, to encourage energy flow and promote natural healing. It's an effective therapy that you can try out at home.

One easy one to find is the heart acupoint, which is great for relieving anxiety, helping you sleep better and calming the nervous system. Hold your hand palm face up and draw a little imaginary line from between your ring and little fingers to your wrist. This acupoint lies at the junction of this line and the wrist crease. Hold your wrist in the opposite hand and gently apply pressure with your thumb. Hold it for about a second, then release it and pump it like this for about 60 seconds.

Massage is one of the most therapeutic and restorative treatments, with well-documented health benefits. Firstly, massage helps boost circulation and increases blood supply to your internal organs. It's been shown to decrease levels of stress hormones, and can help with panic attacks.

A regular massage can help relax you. Ideally, try and find yourself a mobile masseur as they come to your house. To give yourself (or someone else) a full body massage, you'll need about six drops of essential oil blended with four teaspoons (about 20ml) of a carrier oil such as grapeseed, sweet almond oil, soya oil, peach or apricot kernel oils. A regular massage at bedtime could help you unwind.

Reiki: this is a lovely gentle touch massage. Its name means 'universal life force' in Japanese. It works on the premise that if your body's flow of energy stagnates, illness and low moods – and sleep problems – may occur. The practitioner uses gentle hands-on massage, which gives you a lovely warm feeling as the heat moves through your body. It's incredibly relaxing and you may find yourself sleeping better after a session.

Meditation and hypnotherapy: these mind-body therapies are believed to work on the premise that by relaxing the mind you can help heal the body. Aromatherapy can help relieve muscular pain, reduce anxiety and promote relaxation. Hypnotherapy has been found to help with pain control, anxiety, IBS and asthma. Both can help with insomnia.

Herbalism: practitioners have long used valerian as a sedative, and many scientific trials back this up. One study showed that valerian extract has positive effects on patients' quality of sleep, with remarkably few side effects, and concluded that it could be recommended for mild insomnia.

Reflexology: this complementary therapy works on the feet or hands to help heal the whole patient. The theory is that the soles of the feet and palms of the hands mirror the body's internal organs. It is also diagnostic – the reflexologist can detect subtle changes in specific points on the feet. By gently manipulating the areas, they can treat the corresponding organ or system of the body and restore natural equilibrium.

Tools for better slumber

Here are a few ideas that may be worth investigating to help you get a good night's sleep.

Try 'white noise' – which is similar to the sound of rushing air. It is said to mask noise with a natural sound, thereby helping you sleep. Try it on CDs, available from www.purewhitenoise.com or look into machines such as The Marsona 1288 Programmable Sound Conditioner, available at www.justnaturalstuff.co.uk

A Seasonal Affective Disorder lightbox and Bodyclock product may help regulate your circadian rhythms. See www.boots.com or www.lumie.com

Meditate to the best audio CDs:
Restful Sleep by Paul McKenna at
www.amazon.co.uk or www.mckenna-direct.com

www.dreamessentials.com has sleep-promoting products that include relaxing CDs, eye masks and alarm clocks to help you wake to natural light

Find pillows, mattresses and other bedding said to aid sleep at www.nikkenuk.com

Try Snore Calm® anti-snoring strips and sprays at www.britishsnoring.co.uk or Helps Stop Snoring Spray at www.boots.com

A wide selection of CDs for relaxation at sleep time is available at www.newworldmusic.com 01986 891600

Best mattresses/beds/pillows
Try www.back2.co.uk for the best mattresses, pillows and sleep aids

www.backinaction.co.uk
020 7930 8309

For back and neck friendly pillows try
The Pillow Company on www.waterpillow.co.uk

The anti-snore Prelude Snorban Pillow is said to
help snorers, and their bed partners, by helping
to keep airways open. Available from Argos at
www.argos.co.uk

www.johnlewis.com has a great range of quality
beds and mattresses (and is also good for
blackout blinds)

Natural Remedies

For nutritional supplements and alternative
remedies try the following:

www.bioforce.co.uk
01294 277344

www.bachfloweressences.co.uk
020 8780 4200

www.hollandandbarrett.com 0870 606 6605

www.solgar.co.uk

www.boots.com

Aromatherapy oils/products

The following produce essential oils and/or specialist sleep-promoting formulations and beauty products:

Aromatherapy Associates:
www.aromatherapyassociates.com
020 8569 7030

Tisserand: www.tisserand.com 01273 325666

Comfort & Joy: www.comfortandjoy.co.uk
01367 850278

Origins: www.origins.com 0800 731 4039

Elemis: www.elemis.com

Sleep disorders

Insomnia is only one part of the picture. Sometimes there are other medical conditions disrupting sleep:

Obstructive sleep apnoea (OSA)

This is a severe sleep disorder associated with high blood pressure, heart attacks and strokes. It can be life-threatening. OSA causes sufferers to stop breathing repeatedly during their sleep – often several hundred times per night. About 180,000 people in the UK are affected.

Symptoms or warning signs may include high blood pressure, weight gain, excessive sweating at night and loss of sex drive.

Sufferers often snore, may notice their heart pounding at night and tend to wake up feeling exhausted, despite sleeping through the night.

OSA is caused by a lack of muscle tone in the upper airway that causes the airway to collapse. It doesn't happen during the day because you have sufficient muscle tone to keep the airway open, allowing for normal breathing.

OSA can range in severity. A specialist sleep study, involving a night in hospital where equipment will be used to monitor the quality of your sleep, is the best way to diagnose and assess the problem.

Losing weight can often be beneficial. The problem may also be treated with a mouth breathing oral guard to keep airways functioning normally, or with a CPAP machine with mask, which the patient uses at night. In severe cases, surgery may be necessary.

For more information see your GP or contact the British Snoring & Sleep Association on www.britishsnoring.co.uk

Restless leg syndrome (nocturnal myoclonus)

Also known as Ekbom syndrome after the doctor who first described it in the forties, this is a disorder characterised by pain or crawling sensations in the legs at night.

It is thought that one in 10 people is affected. Symptoms include jerking or kicking, aching sensations in your legs or leg pain at night. Often sufferers wake up with sore or aching muscles, and feel sleepy the following day.

It's not known what causes restless leg syndrome. It may be an imbalance of brain chemicals or it may be genetic. It often gets worse during times of stress, during pregnancy, after caffeine or alcohol or as a result of iron deficiency.

Sometimes restless leg syndrome arises as a side effect of certain medications. Occasionally it may be a symptom of health conditions such as Parkinson's disease, diabetes, kidney problems and an under-active thyroid.

For mild cases of nocturnal myoclonus, provided there are no serious underlying medical conditions, a warm bath or cold pack and cutting down on caffeine and alcohol could help. In severe cases medication may be needed.

See your GP or contact the Ekbom Support Group, 01702 582 002 or www.ekbom.org.uk for more info.

Narcolepsy and excessive daytime sleepiness

This is a neurological condition that affects the area of the brain that controls waking and sleeping. It is characterised by uncontrollable sleep attacks during the day, and is often accompanied by cataplexy (sudden loss of muscular control).

Sufferers may fall asleep while driving, during physical exertion, when the sufferer gets stressed or even while laughing or crying. They often have difficulty concentrating in the day and feel as if they're walking around in a daze. Often they can't stay awake, however hard they try. They may have vivid dreams or feel they're hallucinating while they're asleep.

About five or six per cent of people are affected – usually young people under 45. It often begins in adolescence.

Studies in California discovered that levels of orexin, a neurotransmitter that is in control of sleep and wakefulness, are very low or even undetectable in sufferers of narcolepsy.

Although there is no cure, the condition can be treated with sleep therapy and regular naps to reduce excessive sleeplessness. Sometimes drugs are prescribed for cataplexy. Regular exercise and stress reduction can help.

For more information see your GP or visit www.narcolepsy.org.uk

Night terrors and sleep walking

Distinct from nightmares, night terrors are simple or short dreams which usually happen soon after going to sleep, early in the night. Someone experiencing a night terror will wake up screaming, thrashing about and may sit upright and staring. Rarely do they have any recollection

Get a Good Night's Sleep

of the dream, whereas a nightmare is often remembered.

Night terrors are more common in children, but tend to run in families. Excessive tiredness, anxiety or stress may cause night terrors, as may eating a large and heavy meal before bedtime.

About two per cent of adults sleep walk, and, as with night terrors, there is rarely any recollection of any dream involved.

Although neither night terrors nor sleepwalking are considered an illness, in severe cases anti-depressants or sedatives may be prescribed. Stimulants such as alcohol and caffeine may exacerbate the problem.

For more info see your GP or visit
www.nightterrors.org

54   • QUICK123 GUIDES TO EVERYTHING •

And finally

Just because you've never considered yourself a naturally good sleeper doesn't mean you're destined for a life of broken nights and daytime exhaustion.

There are a lot of ways to make sure your nights are more refreshing. Overhaul your lifestyle, make small steps to change your diet, start exercising and set aside some time for relaxation.

Having read this guide, you now know the tricks you need to get a good night's sleep. They're not difficult, so use them. They could just change your life.

Goodnight.

Further

• •

Updates to this guide can be found at: www.quick123.co.uk/sleep

On paper
The Good Sleep Guide
by Michael Van Straten (Kyle Cathie, £8.99)

Bodyfoods for Busy People
by Jane Clarke (Quadrille, £14.99) www.bodyfoods.com

The Insomniac's Best Friend:
How To Get A Better Night's Sleep
by Lynda Brown (Thorsons, £9.99)

Insomnia: Take Control of Your Health Naturally
by Ann Redfearn (Gaia Books, £10.99)

The Body Clock Diet
by Lyndel Costain (Hamlyn, £9.99)

On the web
British Chiropractic Association
www.chiropractic-uk.co.uk (0118 950 5950)
Provides information on beds and the best sleep positions.

reading

••••••••••••••••••••••••••••••••••

The London Sleep Centre
www.londonsleepcentre.com (020 7725 0523)
Specialist centre offering diagnosis and treatment to those with
insomnia and other sleep disorders.

The Sleep Council www.sleepcouncil.com (01756 791089)
Provides information on getting a better night's sleep, choosing
a mattress and has the latest research and news on sleep.

The British Sleep Society www.sleeping.org.uk
A professional organisation predominantly for medical,
healthcare and scientific workers who have an interest in sleep
and its medical disorders, as well as the latest research and news.

The Loughborough Sleep Research Centre
www.lboro.ac.uk/departments/hu/groups/sleep/
Provides the latest research and study on sleep.
The Insomnia Research Programme is run from here.

The Mental Health Foundation www.mentalhealth.org.uk
(020 7803 1100)
Provides fact sheets and information on sleep disorders.

Also available from

Quick123™

•GUIDES TO EVERYTHING•

- Get a Good Night's Sleep
- How to Protect Yourself from Identity Theft
- 25 Ways to Boost Your Income
- Get Started On eBay
- Get Out of Debt - and stay out
- Lose a Stone - and keep it off

and many more.....

For a list of titles and products go to
www.quick123.co.uk